FUNNYOSITIES

THE COMIC GEMS OF
CHIC MURRAY

BIRLINN

This edition published in 2019 by
Birlinn Limited
West Newington House
10 Newington Road
Edinburgh
EH9 1QS

First published in 2009 as *Chic Murray's Funnyosities*

www.birlinn.co.uk

ISBN: 978 1 78027 630 4

British Library Cataloguing-in-Publication Data
A catalogue record for this book is available from the
British Library

Designed and typeset by Mark Blackadder

Printed and bound by Bell & Bain Limited, Glasgow

CONTENTS

This book is dedicated to Iain and Laura
from Anatomy – you know why

INTRODUCTION

Chic Murray was quite simply one of the best comedians ever to have come out of Scotland. Not that his fame was limited to his native land. After early years treading the boards with his wife, Maidie (their famous double act was known as 'The Tall Droll with the Small Doll' – he being six foot three, she four foot eleven), Chic went on to become well-known throughout Britain, both on stage and TV. He also made memorable appearances in films, most notably in Bill Forsyth's wonderful *Gregory's Girl*.

Chic's brand of humour, based on a hilariously surreal view of the world, was truly innovative and appealed not just to his countless fans. The writer Stuart Hepburn has called his humour 'exquisitely drawn and flinty sharp'. He was affectionately known as 'the Comedian's

Comedian', and during his long career he received unstinting praise from a whole host of comic colleagues, including Billy Connolly, Robin Williams, Spike Milligan, Barry Cryer, Robbie Coltrane and Ronnie Barker, to name just a few. Michael Caine does a wonderful impersonation of him.

It's a testament to Chic's talent – timeless in its universal appeal – that a hundred years after his birth his humour continues to make us laugh, reaching new audiences who weren't even born when he died in 1985. Witness to his enduring legacy are the acclaimed play by Stuart Hepburn – *Chic Murray: A Funny Place for a Window,* starring Dave Anderson, Maureen Carr and Brian James O'Sullivan, which has enjoyed sell-out performances in 2019. Coincidentally, Chic, 'the Big Man', has been immortalised in bronze along with Billy Connolly, 'the Big Yin', thanks to the unstinting efforts of Òran Mór owner Colin Beattie, who commissioned a fantastic statue by David Annand of Chic (on a seesaw with Billy!) And there's his inclusion in the Comedy Carpet in Blackpool, which was opened by his old pal Ken Dodd, not to mention the

INTRODUCTION

work of the Chic Murray Appreciation Society, founded by Rob Ellen on facebook, and much else besides.

This book features many of Chic's very best one-liners, as well as longer jokes and stories too. Whether you're already an inveterate 'Chicoholic' or have yet to discover his unique comic voice, we hope you enjoy it. It's our privilege to share it with you.

Here's to you, Dad, and here's to the next hundred years!

Douglas and Annabelle

FUNNYOSITIES

What is a Scot? This is a question people keep asking me. I can only say a Scot is somebody who keeps the Sabbath and everything else he can lay his hands on. Joking apart, is the Scot really mean? Are all these stories about Aberdeen true? Well, you can judge for yourself. My father was an Aberdonian and a more generous man you couldn't wish to meet. I have a gold watch that belonged to my father. He sold it to me on his deathbed, so I wrote him a cheque.

Is the Scotsman's thriftiness hereditary? Maybe my uncle can help to answer that question. An American lady in hospital needed three blood transfusions to save her life, and my uncle, being the unselfish man that he is, volunteered to be a blood donor. For the first pint, she gave him $50. For the second, $25. And, for the third pint . . . nothing! So you see – it's in the blood.

When I was a kid, my mother hired a woman to push my pram and I've been pushed for money ever since. But, please don't think we are all just money grabbers in Scotland. We realise that money isn't everything – women are the other 5 per cent! After all, what is money? The Mint makes it first and we've got to make it last. The Scot is not as tight-fisted as some people make out. I read in a newspaper last week where a Scotsman had actually offered £50,000 to the first man to swim the Atlantic in gumboots. And in business, the Scot has few equals. My father once told me that my grandfather was one of the most successful men in Britain, so much so, that one businessman in London wrote to him asking the secret of his success. My grandfather wrote back and told him it was all a matter of 'brain food' and that he would give him a correspondence course at 2 guineas per lesson. Each week my grandfather sent him a pair of kippers which cost him 2 shillings and for which he received 2 guineas by return. But about six months and 48 guineas later, he received a letter which read:

Dear Mr Murray,

I have had a feeling for some months now that two guineas is rather a high price to pay for a pair of kippers. I am now almost convinced that the charge is much too high.

Yours faithfully

Cedric Smithers

My grandfather was equal to these aspersions. He wired back: 'Imperative you continue course. Undoubtedly, it's beginning to show reults.'

Of course thriftiness is not the only characteristic that the Scot has to take a bit of stick for. Take the kilt, for instance. He is very proud to wear the kilt and display his clan tartan, but he's all too often the butt of the alien's tongue. I wore my kilt last week down south in enemy-held territory when I was approached by the usual inquisitive young lady who wanted to know the age-old secret. I thought, 'Here we go again!' She said, 'Pardon me, Mr Murray, but my friends and I would like to know what is worn under the kilt?' I said, 'Madam, nothing is worn. Everything is in fine working order!' I think it's about time we did something about this question. Could see-through sporrans, perhaps, be the answer? . . . Just a thought.

One cannot mention the Scot without mentioning whisky, the national drink. There are only two rules for drinking whisky: first, never take whisky without water and, second, never take water without whisky. The Scot is very proud of being able to hold his drink. I remember being out with a friend of mine one night, and we had a real ball. The next morning I met him, I said, 'You had a real skinful last night. Did you manage to get home all right?' He said, 'I was getting home fine when a big policeman tramped over my fingers.' Then there was the Scot in London on holiday who had been out on the bevy. He was making his way home when he was set upon by a gang of thugs. The Scot, a born fighter, and with ample whisky courage, put up a very stubborn resistance. But after a long and bloody struggle, he was finally overpowered. The gang leader, after such a battle, was expecting rich booty, but after turning his pockets inside out, he found only one measly sixpenny piece. 'Sixpence! Only sixpence after a stramash like that!' But his mate sagely commented, 'Maybe we're lucky. Imagine what it would've been like if he'd had a shilling!'

Still, Scotland has much to recommend it. For example, we gave golf to the world. St Andrews is the home of golf, but I'm sure St Andrew never played it or he'd never have become a saint. I don't like to boast, but I'm a very accurate golfer myself – straight down the middle, that's me. It will give you an idea of how accurate I am when I tell you that last week I lost my first ball in ten years . . . the string broke. I was taught golf by an old professional, a real purist with everything done according to the book. I'll never forget my first lesson. I went onto the tee and he gave me a seven iron. I was so nervous, I could hardly hold the club. He placed the ball on the tee. Then, taking my courage in both hands, I swung through the ball and, to my amazement, it flew through the air, right onto the green and rolled into the cup. As I waited for congratulations, the pro said, 'Naw, naw, laddie. That'll nae do at a' – ye're using the wrang grip!'

What else do we have to blow about in

Scotland? – The bagpipes, what else? Many a hungry garrison has been relieved to hear the skirl of the pipes in the distance. How is it then, that so many people can't stand them? And how does a piper learn to play? I took up the bagpipes once. I was blowing away merrily, marching round the room, when my wife came upstairs. 'You'll have to do something about that noise,' she said. What could I do? So I took my shoes off and marched around in my stocking feet. Oh, you have to come and go in life.

Well, I hope I've enlightened some of you foreigners who have been reading this. Remember that Scotland has produced many things that make this world a better place. She gave the world chloroform invented by Simpson, penicillin invented by Fleming and 'Funnyosities' invented by Chic Murray. What more could you want? (In answer to the last question, please send on a Rolls Royce Silver Phantom and, in return, I will write on a plain postcard a minimum of twenty words telling you exactly why I like it.)

P.S. In case of fire, cut along the dotted line.

GAGS, ONE-LINERS, SPOONERISMS, PUNS AND WITTICISMS

KISSES, KITH AND KIN

In a recent interview with a national daily newspaper, I stated that 'Chic was a master of absurdities but never smutty'. And the moral of this little observation is, don't conduct an interview over the telephone! To my horror, the following day, the quotation had morphed into a wonderful oxymoron, 'Chic was a master of obscenities, but never smutty'. Undoubtedly, Chic loved the turn of a pretty ankle, and whilst he admired the fairer sex all his life, his observational skills and humour paid close attention to the subject matter. He took no prisoners!

He'd make someone a wonderful stranger.

'Archie, tell me, am I the first girl you've ever made love to?'

'Och! Don't tell me you're the same lassie I met behind the hangar at Glasgow airport all these years ago?'

'Am I the only man in your life, darling?'

'Of course you are, you silly billy. Why does every stupid man ask the same damn-fool question?'

She'd been married five times before and the groom, six times. The wedding invitation warned, 'This is no amateur affair.'

Two of my girlfriends had a duel over me to see who would get me. One of them got me on the leg and the other got me in the arm.

I told my girlfriend to slip into something cool. Ten minutes later, I found her in the fridge.

'Do you fancy going to the Friday disco tomorrow?'

'I can't, Derek, I'm getting married in the afternoon.'

'Well, what about Saturday, then?'

'Oh! Here comes that boy you've fancied for ages, Aggie.'

'Well, I'll drop my hanky . . . dammit! – I've come out without one! What else can I drop?'

My new girlfriend told me she's got mirrors right round her bedroom and more mirrors on the ceiling. I was dead excited when she invited me round. She asked me to bring a bottle. So I ran round with a bottle of window cleaner.

There are three other things besides sex. Nothing you'd want, of course.

I started going with this girl and, in no time at all, I asked for her hand. So she gave it to me . . . right across my left ear.

I was caught passionately embracing a distant cousin. Somebody reminded me that we were distantly related. I replied, 'Aye, aye! – But all I'm doing is just shortening the distance.'

I was dancing with my girlfriend when I said, 'This is a nice dance floor.'

'Why don't you try it then, and get off my feet?'

'You know, darling, I've always admired you from afar.'

'Mmm, that's about the right distance.'

'You remind me of the sea.'

'Oh, why is that? Is it because you see me as a little rough, tempestuous, even?'

'No. I only have to look at the sea to feel sick.'

'What's the difference between Rice Crispies and sex?'

'Dunno.'

'Well, why not pop round for breakfast tomorrow?'

An Eskimo couple got engaged. On the way to the church, they had an argument and so she broke it off . . .

The bride wore a lemon dress. The groom was a sucker.

I always wished her eyes were close to mine. But unfortunately, they're just close to each other.

'My boyfriend slings a rope round my neck and drags me along. Do you think he's serious?'

'No, he's just stringing you along.'

She wasn't all there, of course, but what was there was enough to make it interesting.

I've got this friend named Alec. He's just cricket daft. Cricket! Cricket! Bloody cricket! It's all he seems to dream about. I asked him once, 'Do you ever dream about women?'

'What!' he replied, 'and miss my chance to bat?'

'How could you make love to that woman behind my back?

'Oh! With great difficulty, if you want the truth.'

What a vicious rumour! The music teacher and I were only trying on our Adam and Eve costumes.

'Y'know, darling, I believe our love can last till the end of time.'

'Yeah. There's still fifteen minutes each way to play before they go to a penalty shoot-out.'

'It's amazing. My husband hasn't spent a single penny in the last six months.'

'What's he been doing?'

'Six months.'

The wife's started doing bird impressions. Aye, she watches me like a hawk.

'Do you believe in love at first sight?'

'Blimey yes! Look at the time and money you save!'

'It's hard to believe, but there's now an abortion clinic in Dublin.'

'Oh?'

'Yes, but there's a waiting list. Ten months.'

The minister was taking details of the lady's recently born babies before their christening.

'And so what names do you wish to call your twins at the baptismal font, Ms McKay?'

'Hitler and Mussolini.'

'Goodness me, Ms McKay, why is that?'

'Vicar, I'm an honest lassie! They're both bastards!'

'Quick – grab that pram!'

'But it's not got our child in it.'

'Stop prevaricating, you silly woman! It's a far better pram.'

'I just want to teach the lassie what's right and what's wrong.'

'Well, I'll do a deal with you, Jock. Why don't you teach her what's right, and just leave the rest to me?'

'My plastic surgeon altered my nose.'

'Why? Your nose was OK the way it was.'

'Yeah, but he caught me in bed with his wife.'

'Does your boyfriend ever discuss UNO?'

'God! He never talks about anything else!'

Being born outside Matlock is a sight better than being born out of wedlock. But, come to think about it, there's arguments both ways.

'Shall we please get married, darling?'

'Sorry. That's a bit of a "no-no". Actually, it's completely impossible.'

'Oh, for Heaven's sake, why, sweetheart?'

'I can't begin to express to you just how utterly repulsive you are.'

'Darling! – You're so romantic. Why didn't you say that before?'

'Do you find me attractive, John?'

'Well, at moments like this, it's good to be on an aircraft.'

'Why sweetie?'

'They have paper bags readily available.'

I was kissing my girlfriend when, all of a sudden, I got a lump in my throat. She'd been chewing on a pickled onion.

'Excuse me, miss, you've dropped your hankie.'

'I know. I've finished with it.'

'Well . . . could I hold your hand?'

'No thanks. I can hold it myself. Besides, it's not heavy.'

'But I must tell you, you've got the most beautiful eyes . . .'

'Yeah, they came with the face. Goodbye.'

'Pardon me, may I have the next dance?'

'Certainly – if you can find a partner.'

As a Grenadian, I wanted to settle down with my girlfriend – a lovely English nudist/naturist – in the West Indies. It was an awful shame. She refused to marry me – too much sun, she said. All she wanted, she said, was a white wedding!

Marriage is a bit like having a bath. After you get used to it, you find it's not so hot.

I first met my wife in the Tunnel of Love. She was digging it.

I just bought the wife a Jaguar. It's been a great investment. Only last week, it bit her leg off.

'How did you get your car stuck in the river?'
   'The wife kept nagging me to dip the headlights.'

'Where's my tea?' I asked the wife.
   'You're late, so I had to keep it warm for you.'
   'Where is it then?'
   'In the fire.'

'Good evening, madam. I'm from the environmental Health Department of Glasgow City Council – Pest Control Division.'
   'Aye, well ye'd better come in. He's no back frae the pub yet.'

'How's your good wife?'
   'How the Hell would I know? I only have the one.'

My wife's a redhead. Oh, you should see her! – No hair, just a red head!

'I'm homesick,' I said to the wife the other day.
    'Don't be silly,' she said, 'this is your home.'
    'I know. And I'm sick of it.'

My wife's quite a good artist. Recently she painted a civil servant in the workplace and – good for her! – it won a prize in the still life section.

'Have you brought your bag with you?'
    'Nah! The wife's on night duty this week.'

Dan's wife never knew whether she was coming or going with him. It was hardly surprising, though. He had this removal van and kept driving up and down the street.

A man returned home early to surprise his wife. But instead, she surprised him as he found her in the marital bed with two men. 'Hello, Hello,' he said in a confused state, whereupon his wife, popping her head above the blankets, countered, 'Oh, so you're not speaking to me, then?'

Marriage brings music into your life. But eventually most blokes get fed up playing second fiddle.

My wife's a hellish driver. It's just one accident after the other. As if to help, she's now paid (from the housekeeping money, I should add!) – to have one side of her car painted blue, leaving the other side red so that, with a bit of luck, witnesses will contradict each other.

My wife went to the beauty parlour for a mud pack. She looked great for a couple of days until the mud fell off. But she's a classy girl. All her tattoos are spelt right.

This poor woman was suffering from a really nasty cold. She asked her husband how could she prevent it from going from her head into her chest. I must say he solved the problem in no time by simply tightening a ligature round her throat.

My marriage was very unhappy although we're still married. I once hit the wife on the head with a chair. 'Why did you do that?' the police asked. I replied, 'Because I couldn't lift the piano.' But when she recovered, she flattened me by smashing me over the head with an oak leaf. The oak leaf was the centrepiece of our dining room table.

Archie didn't mind the wife leaving him. But he was a bit depressed when he went home to his mother to find her trying to rub her name off his birth certificate.

'You should have seen the wife's face when I brought the babysitter round on Tuesday!'
   'What was wrong with that?'
   'Well, we don't have any children yet.'

'I decided when I got married, I would arrange the ceremony at four in the afternoon.'

'Why did you want to tie the knot so late?'

'I suppose I sussed that if it didn't work out, at least the whole day wouldn't be wasted.'

'The wife and I haven't spoken to each other for two years.'

'Oh. Did you have a row?'

'No. We just can't think of anything to say to each other.'

Ian point blank refuses to take his wife out. He says it's a matter of principle. He just doesn't want to mix with married women.

'It's hellish serious . . . do you know the penalty for bigamy? Yes or No?

'Maybe, but go on.'

'You get two mothers-in-law.'

The prisoner in the dock had thrown his mother-in-law through the window, three floors up. The judge, in summarising the evidence and passing sentence, said, 'That was an act of sheer folly which could have been very dangerous. Someone could well have been passing underneath.'

'I would like a blind dog, please, for my mother-in-law.'

'Sorry, sir. I think you mean a guide dog.'

'No. I mean a blind dog! If the dog could see her, it would go straight for the throat!'

'I had to take the dog to the vet. It bit my mother-in-law.'

'Are you getting it put down?'

'God, no! It's in to get its teeth sharpened.'

That uncle of mine is a born loser. You know if, by some fluke, he cornered the market for mistletoe, what's the betting they'd go on and cancel Christmas?

My sister keeps pigeons. It's not the expense that worries her, it's the overheads.

My poor sister fell asleep on her water bed. Then the house went on fire. She was poached to death.

FUNNYOSITIES

When we were expecting our second baby, I had to break the news to our son. 'A stork is going to fly round in circles,' I told him, 'and drop a baby down the chimney right onto your Mama's bed.' 'I hope it doesn't frighten the life out of her,' he replied, 'she's having one herself.'

A father told his son that the newly arrived baby had been dug up under a gooseberry bush. The following day, he spotted the boy with a dirty spade and mucky boots. 'Oh,' said the father, have you been digging for another baby?'

'Nah!' replied the bairn, 'I was just putting the other one back.'

Dad was unusual as he had just this one tooth in the middle of his mouth. I used to beg him to have it removed and to get fitted with dentures. But – no! – he always refused. He said he needed it for central eating.

'You know, your daughter was hellish honest with me. She told me all her faults.'

'Don't be daft, Jimmy. Come on! – You were only going out with her for a month!'

My brother-in-law's a man who can liven up any party . . . as long as he stays away, that is.

'Do you know the Barber of Seville, son?
    'Yeah, I do, Dad.'
    'Well get your bloody hair cut.'

'Don't get supercilious with me, son!'
    'What does that mean, Dad?'
    'I've no idea but it's worth at least eighteen points at Scrabble.'

My grandfather was an utter genius. He even invented a cure from which there was no disease. Unfortunately, Granny caught the cure.

Och! Get down off that gas cooker in your ankle-length bloomers, Grannie! You're far too old to be riding the range.

'Grandpa, can you croak like a frog?'
    'I don't think so son. But why do you ask?'
    'Well ah heard Ma saying, once the auld yin croaks, I'm taking the bairns to Disneyland.'

THE WORK BLUES VERSUS THE GREENBACKS

Chic worked hardest on his scripts. After all, one of the remarkable distinctions between him and the comedic fraternity was that all his material was his own in a world where script writers didn't exist. In any case, as Billy Connolly commented, 'Who the Hell could have written for Chic?' He was known to refresh his memory, on occasions, sitting on a lavatory seat, but, even then, nothing was ever remembered verbatim. No two performances were the same, which gave his humour a spontaneity and freshness that others could only envy. On the money front, it would be fair to say the said Chic was 'careful' – (very, very careful!)

'I'm going to have to do something to keep the bills down'

    'Your best bet is a heavy paperweight.'

I don't care if he was the head of the light brigade. There will be no charging in here!

Is it true? I heard all tall detectives were paid by the yard?

The hotel was that posh, the waiters were giving me tips.

'Can you spare me a fiver, sir? I've only got six months to live.'

    'Och, never mind! – It'll soon pass.'

'Can you swap this toilet roll for five Senior Service?'

    'What on earth for?'

    'The visitors never arrived.'

'We'll have some champagne with the meal. Make sure it's the right voltage.'

'Ahem. Does sir not mean vintage?'

'Voltage, I said! Your prices are shocking!'

'Can anyone with money join your poker school?'

'No problem as long as you don't mind being parted from it.'

If you want to know how it feels for a cow when it's being milked, just pop along to your local Inland Revenue Office.

I'm very pleased for my brother Fred. He's got a great new job with the Inland Revenue. He's a terrific pickpocket by profession and they maintain he'll make huge savings on the paperwork.

'My dad took these threatening letters to the police and he was furious when they refused to take any action.'

'Were the threats accompanied by something which could identify where the threats were coming from?'

'Oh yes. The Inland Revenue.'

The trouble with these people that work for the tax authorities is – honestly! – they drive you to the drink. Then, what do they do? You've just raised your glass for a wee bit of comfort when they tell you they've increased the duty again!

'Are you superstitious, Henry?'

'Not at all. That's just ignorant, primitive bunkum.'

'Great! Lend me £13 then.'

I took my salary to the bank. I had to. It was too small to go by itself. I'm going to have to get a better paid job. Right now, three companies are after me, the electricity company, the gas company and the water board.

THE WORK BLUES VERSUS THE GREENBACKS

Some people have trouble meeting their bills. But not me. Oh no! My trouble is dodging them. Aye, they say that money talks. All it ever says to me is 'Cheerio!' And it never tells you when it's coming back. Never!

Next year, I'm going to make a strenuous effort to live within my means – even if I have to borrow money to do it, because I'm not lazy. Far from it! Hard work fascinates me. I can watch it for hours. But, at the end of the day, ask yourself, what is a rich man? After all there's not a jot of difference between a rich man and a poor man. Think about it! – All he is, is a poor man with loads of money.

It was about August last year that I realised there was insanity in the family. One after another, they wrote to me wanting money, of all things!

I was stony broke so I wrote to my father. 'Dear Dad,' I said, 'I'd love to hear from you more often – even if it's only for five or ten pounds.'
He wrote back, 'Dear Son, I'm sorry I couldn't enclose any money in this letter as, unfortunately, the envelope was already sealed.'

'My staff have no problems over money. It works very well actually.'
  'Oh, how do you manage that?'
  'It's fairly straightforward. You just don't pay them enough to cause any problems in the first place.'

'OK, OK. I do realise that we're eighteen weeks behind with the rent. But I promise you this – it'll all be different next week.'
  'How do you work that one out?'
  'Well, for a start we'll be owing nineteen weeks.'

If the price of jelly babies goes up any more, I'm going to see if I can get them on the family allowance.

THE WORK BLUES VERSUS THE GREENBACKS

If the present rise in prices keeps going at this rate, the good old days will be last week.

Honestly. I wouldn't think twice. I would give £1000 to be a millionaire.

'I've been a foreman now for fourteen years.'
'Crikey! That's a helluva long time doing nothing.'

I passed the minister the other day. 'Hello, Reverend,' I said, 'still on a one-day week?'

This Irish cat burglar thinks he's good. He's pleased with himself because he's stolen fifteen cats this week alone.

For a while there was a massive exodus of Irish, emigrating to China. They were looking for work in the paddy fields.

The union democratically decided to act on a show of hands but they insisted, quite properly, that everyone had to be blindfolded first.

Now, look, my friends, my grandfather was a politician. My father was a politician. I'm a politician. And, if I have anything to do with it, my son won't work either!

Last week I landed a cracking job. It made my mother very happy. She said, if I worked a week, she'd put a bed in my room. If I worked two weeks, she'd put a mattress on the bed. And if I managed to work a full month, she'd ask the other six fellows to move out.

Isn't it funny how some girls always get salary increases after every office party?

My boss is unbelievably narrow-minded. When he has a fresh idea, it comes out folded.

I've given up the taxi game, definitely, this time. I'm sick of folk talking behind my back.

When these politicians keep telling us that they just want to serve the public, us farmers know exactly what they mean. Whoever heard of a bull that doesn't serve the cow?

THE WORK BLUES VERSUS THE GREENBACKS

Mike lives by his wits. That explains the half-starved look on his face.

'Did you ask for a rise today, as you told me?'
'No, in all the excitement of getting the sack, it went clean out of my head.'

'I'm giving that Jimmie Brown a going-away present.'
'Oh, I didn't know he was going. Where's he off to?'
'Dunno. But he'll take the hint.'

'I'm working eighteen hours a day.'
'Ach! Never mind, a part-time job is better than nothing.'

I just love driving hearses. And, of course, you've got the added bonus – no back-seat drivers!

'It's getting more and more difficult for me to believe you're working late through overtime.'
'Why?'
'You're unemployed.'

'I know how you can completely do away with unemployment.'

'Rubbish! No economist has ever succeeded in that!'

'Yes, but if you have no employment, then you've got no unemployment!'

I told this member of staff that in my view, he was 'going places'. Then I gave him his P45 and fired him. It was just to make absolutely sure.

The hardest jobs for the foreman in the stocking factory were bringing the workforce to heel and getting them to toe the line.

I see there's a new column that's started in the paper. It's called 'Sits vacant'. Come to think of it, that describes Alec exactly.

Sammy's not much of a ventriloquist. He's got it all wrong – he speaks his lines while his dummy drinks a glass of water.

'I have a lot of friends in the show business world. Take Johnnie Beattie with whom I have so much in common. We're both incredibly common.'

I have this pal of mine. His only claim to fame was falling off a camel when he was a bairn. There's no point in mentioning Billy Connolly's name. He's had enough bad publicity recently.

I tried my hand on stage as a comic. I was so low on the bill, even the dogs got at me. And some nights there was no applause at all. None! Not one clap! I'd go back to my dressing room and cry. Then the manager would come in with the takings, which was a comfort because we could cry together.

I joined a Shakespearian company. The owner loved *Hamlet* but always insisted on playing the king. He was a bit paranoid, though – always on the look-out in case someone trumped him. But he appeared consistently to move the audience . . . directly towards the first available exit.

DRINKING WITH THE FEET UP WHILST OTHERS STAND UP AND SOME FALL DOWN

Chic had a fair idea of both these activities. Nothing brought him greater contentment than writing scripts in the sun. (The sun was a beneficial therapy to counter psoriasis, which afflicted him during his life.) As a wonderful observer of aberrant human behaviour, Chic loved a drink, and the couthier the watering place, the better he enjoyed it. He was instantly recognised in whatever watering hole, he ventured into, and he thought it was 'somewhat rude' to refuse a small refreshment (or two) from his admirers!

I've got to hand it to them. It only rained twice on my week's break in Blackpool – once for four days and the other time, for three.

Glasgow is lucky having all these entertainment units. Whenever they get bored, they can just drive anywhere within the city boundaries and dig a hole.

I was staying in this fancy hotel in London. Yes, I got back quite late but then I noticed this sign saying, 'All dogs must be carried.' Is that not daft? Where are you supposed to grab a stray dog in the West End after midnight?

The Irish duck hunters returned despondently without a single bird in the bag.

'Maybe we're not flinging the dogs high enough,' one of them thoughtfully suggested.

At the airport, travelling abroad on holiday, I said, 'Crikey! I don't half miss our piano!'

'Why?'

'The passports and flight tickets are on top of it.'

Two elderly lady friends were cruising to their holiday destination at 35,000 feet when one of them, looking down at the cloud base below, remarked, 'Wouldn't it be perfectly dreadful if you and I fell out?'

'Och!' – the other replied – 'we've been friends for far too long for that to happen.'

'I can't make my mind up where to go,' the flustered but wealthy lady said to her travel agent.

'Look,' he said, 'I'll leave you with this globe. You take your time and I'll see how you're getting on and where you've decided to go in ten minutes or so.' After quarter of an hour, he returned. 'Well, Mrs Prendergast?' he enquired indulgently.

'I'm not at all happy, Mr Smith. Could you give me another globe, please!'

An American tourist saw Union Jacks for sale. 'Aw! How cute are they? Give me six, please, and do you have them in any other colours?'

'What can you do in a seaside boarding house that you can't do at home?'

'Well you can remove sand from your belly button, for starters!'

I booked into a hotel that overlooked a lake. But they didn't tell you that it also overlooked good beds, good food and running water. And they told me the rooms were air-conditioned. Every half-hour a bell-boy came up and sprayed the place with a 'Flit' gun. The hot and cold running water was hot in the summer and cold in the winter. But I have to admit, they did have running water. The roof leaked.

I climbed into bed in this Bed and Breakfast establishment. I noticed a sign above the headboard which read, 'Sleep here and the angels watch over you.' All I know is that two of them bit me during the night. And there was no heating. It was so cold, I woke up halfway through the night, disturbed by the chattering noise of my false teeth on the bedside table.

'You should have seen the hotel I stayed in on holiday in Spain!'

'Why? What was so special?'

'It was finished!'

'I went up to this fellow in Paris. I couldn't resist it – I gave him the works, "Vive la France", I said, "Maurice Chevalier, fermez la porte!" I could have gone on, actually.'

'Was he quite surprised?'

'Yes, as it happens. He was Dutch.'

Don't put too much ice in it. It takes up too much room.

A case of your finest malt whisky, please. And two cases of assault and battery. Thank you.

'You'll never believe it. We had a drink on the manager after closing time!'

'Was it good? What was it like?'

'Not bad. The drink was great but it was a wee bit uncomfortable.'

I admit I spent a fortune on wild women, booze and gambling. The rest, I just spent foolishly.

I've got this Special Reserve vatted malt whisky. And, honestly, you never get a hangover from it the next day. Oh no! – You get that the same night.

Give him two dashes of ink and, believe me, Fred gets blotto.

I'm very proud to be standing here before you. I never dreamt I would sober up in time.

'Right, Paddy, I'll see you tonight – God love you, mah bhoy! – in O'Malley's Bar, then?'
    'No bother, Michael! And if you don't see me, feel around a bit. The sawdust's pretty deep there.'

'If you're not drunk, what are you doing languishing there in the gutter?'
    'Sorry, officer. I just found this parking space and sent the wife home to get the car.'

I've heard it's said that alcohol is a slow poison. But that begs the question, who's in a hurry? And what about water? If it can rust iron, just think what it's doing to your stomach!

'By Jove! Hic! Now, that's what I call a decent-sized glass of gin and tonic.'

'Och! Sober Up! That's a goldfish bowl, you lush!'

'Oh really? I wondered why the slice of lemon kept leaping out of my mouth!'

'These green little ice cubes . . . most unusual and dashed cute. Good show!'

'Sorry, sir. Unfortunately, we ran out of ice. They're frozen peas.'

I tend to invite diminutive guests to my parties. There's the hidden advantage that they make the drinks look bigger.

The motorist drove along the motorway at precisely 70mph. He then entered the slow lane, giving perfect hand signals, only to be flagged down by the police.

'Don't worry, sir, we only stopped you to congratulate you on your perfect exhibition of driving.'

'Aye' said the motorist, 'you can't be too careful when you're as pissed as me!'

Two pals went into a busy bar in Glasgow. One approached the barman, 'Two pints o' heavy and two nips of whisky, please.' Turning to his mate, he asked, 'An' what are you going to have, Bert?'

'I'm sorry to see you coming out of that public house,' the minister told one of his congregation.

'Whatever you say, Reverend,' he replied, and heeding his comments, went back in.

I spotted Effie in the pub. I could tell she had class by the way she ordered her pint of heavy and only then did she spit on the sawdust.

Two fall-about drunks were stopped and questioned by the police. 'All right. That's enough!' said the officer, addressing the first, 'Your name and address, please?'

'Hamish Finlay of no fixed abode.' Turning to the other he asked the same question. The second drunk replied, 'Ian Begg of the flat above.'

ILL-DISPOSED TO WELL-BEING

Chic had his share of ill health, some of it caused by his eccentric eating patterns and lifestyle, sometimes living for weeks on end out of suitcases and eating endless greasy spoon breakfasts and, later, fish suppers. Once, in a freezing cold B&B, with snow lying on the street, the landlady caught him trying to open the frosted-up window in the breakfast room. 'Mr Murray, what are you doing?' she asked. 'Just trying to let some heat in,' came the reply. Nonetheless, he was a large strapping man, affectionately billed as 'The Tall Droll with the Small Doll' – a reference to his dainty wife, Maidie, in their heyday as a double act.

'Och, doctor, if I've only got three minutes to live, is there nothing left you can do for me?'

'I suppose I could just about boil you an egg.'

'Doctor, I've got these butterflies in my stomach.'

'Oh, what have you been eating recently?'

'Butterflies.'

'Are you disturbed by improper thoughts during the night?'

'Blimey! – No, doctor. I just love them.'

An elderly pensioner announced to his doctor that he was going to marry a girl of eighteen.

'That could prove fatal,' counselled the doctor.

'Oh well, let her die!' said the old boy.

But the medic could see he was determined, so he suggested, in order to ease the strain, that he took in a lodger as well. Months later the doctor asked him how was his married life.

'Great' said the old fossil, 'the wife's expecting.'

The doctor grinned, 'You followed my advice then, and took in a lodger?'

'Aye,' said the mannie, 'and she's pregnant too!'

'Doctor, I'm losing blood.'
'Now, now, stop panicking! It's just seeping into your coat.

'Medical science has made tremendous strides, you know.'
'Thank God for that! I was glad to see the back of those bloody leeches!'

The doctor rushed through the ward to find out what the hideous noise was all about. He was just in time to see a nurse leaving a screaming patient, a bowl of steaming hot water in her hand as the patient writhed in agony clutching his groin.
'For Chrissakes, nurse, I told you to prick his boil!'

A man, half asphyxiated and clearly in pain, entered the doctor's surgery.

'Help me, doctor! Please! I've just swallowed a cricket ball,' he gagged.

'Howzatt?' said the doctor.

'Och! Don't you bloody start!'

'I'd like a vasectomy, doctor.'

'With a face like yours, honestly, you don't need to bother.'

'Doctor, I've gone over on my ankle. It's sure it's sprained. What should I do?'

'Limp.'

I had a bad cough and went to the doctor, who gave me some medicine. Now I've got a good cough.

'If I give up drink, tobacco and sex, doctor, will I live longer?'

'No, it'll only seem longer.'

'Doctor, I'm losing my hair.'

'Well, why don't you consider having a transplant?'

'Come on! I'd just look daft with a liver or kidney stuck on my baldie heid.'

'Oh, doctor, I'm just a bag of nerves. I can't sleep, I'm that scared!

'Just a suggestion – have you ever tried counting sheep?'

'What! Sheep! – I'm terrified of them.'

'Did you miss a step as you fell down the stairs?'

'I wish to Hell I had! No! – I hit every blinking one of them!'

I must dash off and see my doctor. I've got a nasty complaint called virus X. It was started by some idiot who couldn't spell pneumonia.

Two spoonfuls of strawberry jam is a great cure for seasickness. And it's the only thing that tastes the same going down as it does coming up.

There's a new slimming treatment that's all the rage. They surgically remove all your bones so that not only do you lose a helluva lot of weight, you look so much more relaxed after the operation.

I recently visited my psychiatrist. I told him I couldn't sleep at night. I had these noises in my head. He said that was an impossibility because you can't transmit sound through a vacuum. I retorted that I was nobody's fool, so he said he might know someone who would adopt me.

The doctor examined me thoroughly. He reckoned I was shell-shocked from eating too many peanuts in bed. He suggested I take a long-haul holiday but I couldn't face it. I even get travel sick licking an airmail stamp. He laughed at that and said that there were more accidents in the bath than there were on aeroplanes. So I haven't been in either since.

I wasn't feeling well. I asked my wife to get me something for my liver. She came back from the shops with a pound of onions. So I decided to visit a doctor, someone with a reputation. The one I went to I learnt certainly had a reputation. If you were at death's door, they later told me, he'd pull you through.

The doctor diagnosed that I suffered from a 'falling' stomach. I took no notice until I tripped over it on leaving the surgery.

I remember receiving treatment in America for an ankle injury. But the surgeon said I'd be up and walking in a couple of weeks and I have to admit, he was true to his word. His bill was so astronomic, I had to sell the car.

A Highland 'wifie' from Barra approached her doctor complaining that having had eighteen children, another pregnancy would kill her. But the doctor reasoned with her that she was beyond help because of her religious convictions and her refusal to exercise any form of birth control.

'All I can suggest, Mrs Mackay,' said the doctor, 'is that you stick strictly to the Rhythm Method.'

'Och, don't be daft, doctor,' she replied, 'where am I going to get a ceilidh band at 12 o'clock at night?'

'Doctor, I'm very worried about my laddie. He's a compulsive grape eater.'

'Oh, that's not the end of the world, Mr McLean. Grapes are actually very good for you.'

'Aye, but he eats them off the wallpaper.'

'You shouldn't drink so much. It's not good for you.'

'Ah! – But doctor, look at the exercise I get when I hiccup.'

I don't think that's fair, doctor, to say I take no exercise. For example, I roll my own fags.

I'm proud of my Irish extraction. I got a wisdom tooth removed in Dundalk.

'I've just had all my teeth out.'
    'So, how do you feel?'
    'Never again, I say!'

The dentist's daughter goes around with the worst set in town. But her father makes false teeth so natural that they ache.

Patient: I'd rather have a baby than visit the dentist.
Dentist: No problem, madam, but obviously I'll have to adjust the chair.

WORDPLAY AND PUNS DESIGNED FOR UNWARY, UNSUSPECTING WRONG-FOOTED FALL GUYS

As a wordsmith, Chic excelled in this department. Nothing gave him greater pleasure than wrong-footing the listener, either by misleading them in their interpretation of words, or, ripping words out of context, to shine fresh light on the word's meaning in a wholly unexpected scenario. Add to that, his immaculate sense of timing, and the outcome was a heady cocktail.

'Do you still have your gun?'

'Yeah.'

'Well, keep him covered while I fetch a blanket.'

'I don't recognise this court, your honour. Was it painted blue recently?'

'Where's Uganda?'

'Buried next to my Grandma'

'Excuse me. Do you happen to have a light, mac?'

'Nuh. My only coat's navy blue.'

Motorist: 'I've just run over your cockerel and I'd like to replace him.'

Farmer's wife: 'Fair enough. The hens are round the back.'

'What do you think of Red China?'

'I quite like it on a white tablecloth.'

I had a tragic childhood. My parents never understood me. They were Japanese.

That woman has a tongue on her that can clip hedges.

My neighbour put his budgie in the mincing machine. That's how shredded tweet began.

'I can't tell you how pleased I am.'
   'Why?'
   'Because I'm not a bit bloody pleased, that's why!'

Have you noticed how kitchen sink dramas have just gone down the drain?

He was the first murderer executed in the electric chair. When he heard the verdict, it came as a bit of a shock.

'This shirt', the salesman said, 'will laugh at washing.' He was true to his word. When I got it back from the laundry, its sides were splitting.

An old stager was given a very small part in a play. His total lines consisted of two words – 'It is!' Despite weeks of rehearsing and memorising his lines again and again – 'It is', 'It is,' – when it came to the first night, the old dodderer messed up and said 'Is it?' instead. The producer, demented, yelled, 'You silly damned fool, you've ruined the whole bloody play!'

'Listen, laddie,' replied the oldster, 'I know my part backwards!'

A man was hanging around shiftily some fifty yards removed from the graveside where the deceased was being interred. One mourner, nodding in his direction, said to his companion,

'Have you any idea who that bloke is?'

'I think he's a distant relative,' the friend replied.

When Liam's gang told him to lie low for a while, he cut the legs off his bed.

'How the hell did you arrive in this car in my kitchen?'

'Oh! It's fairly straightforward – you enter, as best you can, through the front door and turn left between the first bedroom and the airing cupboard.'

We had a great membership drive at my golf club last week. Altogether, we managed to drive out no fewer than thirty members!

I walked into the bedroom. The curtains were drawn but the furniture was real.

This lassie, suffering from acne, still managed to win a spot prize at the dance.

I made a stupid mistake last week. But, come to think about it, did you ever hear of a clever mistake?

That man set about establishing a successful flea circus and the whole thing was started from scratch.

Colour television? Aw! – whatever next? Me, I won't begin to believe it until I see it in black and white.

It was a shame. The trombone player's wig fell into his instrument. After that, he spent the entire afternoon blowing his top.

Len's even teeth parted in a smile. However, the odd ones stayed where they were.

And now for some good news for the small farmer – a new breed of small cows.

I was making tea in my pyjamas. I must remember to buy a teapot.

This footman tapped me on the shoulder with his foot . . .

'Did you see my picnickers?'
    'Well, you shouldn't have taken them off in the first place!'

She was called Sugar. Bit of a lump, actually.

I suppose I'm something of a sado-masochist. I'm addicted to agony columns.

What's the matter, baby? Is my little coconut shy?

Aggie used to have an hourglass figure but now all her sand has run down to the bottom.

'You're the wine waiter. You recommend me a good wine.'

'Well why not try the Macon, sir?'

'What? Are you going to pour it over me?'

'Would sir care for an aperitif?'

'What for? Is the steak tough?'

'Fred! Fred! Dad's just gone out again.'

'Oh stop fussing! Just throw some more paraffin over him.'

There's a lovely blonde who's just moved in next door who took my eye. Well, not really! I need it, you see, as it's one of a set.

I said to the landlady, 'Would you call me early?' She let me sleep in but woke me up shouting from the bottom of the stairs, 'Good morning, Early!'

I rang the bell of the bed and breakfast establishment. After a short delay, an upstairs window was flung open. 'Yes, what is it?' said the landlady.

'I would like to stay here,' I shouted up.

'Well just stay there then!' as she slammed the window shut.

'Excuse me,' said the nice man who had nudged me in the bus.

'No problem' I said, 'I'll grant you a full pardon, if it'll help.'

'Thank you for pulling in, sir. This is a standard police spot check.'

'No problem, officer – I've got two pimples and the beginnings of a boil on my bum.'

I was walking down Sauchiehall Street, and then, suddenly, I felt a tap on my shoulder. Imme-diately, I thought to myself, this is a funny place to put a tap.

In the Olympic village, a man in trainers, carrying a long stick, was asked by a stranger: 'Are you a pole vaulter?'

'Nein, I am Deutsche, but how did you know my name was Walter?'

I met this vastly overweight lassie. I asked her, 'What are you doing out here? And here? And here? And here?

Bank manager: 'That's all very well, sir, but do you have collateral?'

Overdraft applicant: 'No. It's just the way I cross my legs.'

'I want some masonry nails, please.'

'How long do you want them?'

'What do you mean? I want them for good!'

'How can you say such a thing?'

'It's quite easy. I just open my mouth and out it pops.'

I once tried smoking hash. But I couldn't get corned beef anywhere.

'I didn't know you were left of centre.'

'I'm not really. It's my tailor. It's the way he styles my trousers.'

'I can beat any heavyweight with just one hand.'

'Oh! Be fair! There's not many one-armed heavyweights going the rounds these days.'

Do you know what kind of lighting they used on Noah's Ark?

Flood lighting.

The Salvation Army had been playing for over half an hour. They ceased playing to rest for a couple of minutes while the band leader asked the growing crowd: 'And what hymn would you like now?'

A throaty woman raised her voice from the back of the crowd: 'Him with the big drum!'

'I never realised you had such a yellow streak.'

'Oh yes! My hairdresser says it's all the rage!'

'I'd like to buy some of those crocodile shoes, please.'

'And what size do the crocodile's feet require?'

Bank robbers, making a hasty exit after a hold-up, ran through freshly poured cement. The police are looking for two hardened criminals.

'Do you know the piano's resting on my foot?'

'Hum or whistle me the tune, then, and I'll give it a try.'

'She carries a torch for Big George.'

'Really? Is she madly in love with him then?'

'Don't be daft! He's a plumber.'

I love food. It's come to the stage where I won't eat anything else.

'He's the luckiest man alive.'

'How?'

'Well, for years he was digging his own grave and then he struck oil!'

'Have you heard the joke about Rothesay?'

'Yes. It's a Bute.'

'I hear the minister's sermon today is on the milk of human kindness.'

'Well I hope it's condensed.'

'Did you hear my last broadcast?'

'Yes. And so it bloody well should be!'

'I'm not a complete idiot, you know!'

'Oh? What part's missing?'

'I come from a very old military family, one of my forebears actually fell at Waterloo!'

'My word!'

'Yes, someone pushed him off platform eleven.'

He's the only welterweight boxer I know who wears ballet shoes. But he maintains that's why he wins on points!

I once made my living with the pen, not writing – breeding pigs.

My parents didn't expect me to be a boxer; they thought I was more of a cocker spaniel.

'You say you're an artist. But you're not! You're just a second-rate boxer!'

'That's your opinion! Being a fighter is the next best thing. I get great pleasure in putting people down on canvas!'

They say my neighbour's an all-action man. He has delirium tremens every morning. But recently, he's being attending deportment classes and possibly in the next few days, he'll be deported.

The boy always wanted to please his father, who had had dozens of previous convictions for burglary. He asked his dad to teach him the rudiments of how to be a successful thief so that he could follow in his father's fingerprints.

I was stopped on the way home the other night. This guy asked me if I wanted a job at the Eagle Laundry. I just flatly refused. After all, who wants to wash eagles for a living?

I heard of an artist's model who was never in the nude for work.

Have you ever tried honeymoon salad? – You know it's lettuce alone without dressing.

This soprano's voice is so high, it's got snow on the top of it.

There was a moth that died of malnutrition. It tried to eat a stripper's costume.

I was once a matinee idol. Oh yes! I used to appear in matinees then revert to being idle.

I suppose my troubles started years ago, when I was only four. I ran away with a circus. But the cops caught up with me and forced me to give it back.

From day one, my parents put me on a raw diet. I ate my breakfast raw. Then my lunch raw. But for dinner, they expected me to put my clothes on.

This poultry farmer told me recently that one of his hens recently kicked a porcelain egg out of her nest. She clucked that no one was going to make a brick layer out of her.

'I've come down from Glasgow to London, for three years running.'
　　'Why don't you drive down or take the train?'

'Darling, I'll give you £750 if you paint me in the nude.'

'Aye, no bother. But I'll need to keep my socks on or I'll have nowhere to put the brushes.'

'I once saw this monkey, you wouldn't believe it, making chips in a restaurant. Just amazing!'

'Must have been a chip monk.'

'Have you got academic leanings, perhaps?'

'No. It's just that I've lost the rubber bit on my left heel.'

'All right, pay attention, class! Name a fish that likes a lot of sleep.'

'Please, sir!' – (hand extended upwards) – 'Kippers.'

'Dad, there's a Black Maria at the door!'

'Well, don't keep her waiting, usher her in, courteously! We'll have no race discrimination in this house.'

'See that man over there? A lie has never passed that man's lips.'

'Gosh! That's amazing!'

'Yup! All his life he's spoken through his nose!'

Oh! – He's a first class athlete, nobody doubts that! But, I'm telling you, man, if the police catch up with him, believe me, he's in for the high jump!

'If you were half a man you would take your wife to the circus.'

'If I were half a man, I'd be in the bloody circus!'

This obsessive would-be vampire was seized in the very act of robbing a blood bank. The police later stated that, after a tip-off, he was caught red-handed.

A pilot radioed Ground Control to announce total engine failure. 'State your height and position,' came the emergency request from the terminal.

'What kind of idiots are they?' the pilot said to his co-pilot, 'I'm five foot ten and I'm still sitting in the front of the bloody aircraft!'

I knew an athlete who was a fantastic sprinter but, at the same time, I never met anybody more stupid. He was unbelievably thick. Once he went for a dope test. He passed.

I walked into this smart gentleman's outfitter for a suit. It was going to be a beauty with hand-stitched lapels. Once he'd finished taking my measurements, the tailor asked me if I wanted buttons on the fly. 'No, no,' I said, 'call me old-fashioned, but I'd rather pay the full price for everything, thank you.'

'If you've finished your glass of port, Cedric, shall we join the ladies?'

'What on earth for? Are they coming apart?'

Fifty-five per cent of men in Toulouse wear their trousers too long but forty-five per cent of men in Toulon wear their trousers too loose.

I met this cowboy with a brown paper hat, brown paper waistcoat and brown paper trousers. The sheriff and his ` posse, however, were after him. He was wanted for rustling.

'Hold me tight, darling.'
    'Hold your tight what?'

My first ambition was to become a coroner but I was put off the idea. Apparently the exams were very stiff.

'No, I honestly think you have one of the finest stamp collections in the country.'
    'Thanks very much. You know what they say, though? Philately will get you nowhere.'

The case of that foreign diplomat is coming up next week. I believe it's an attaché case.

I got this terrible blow-out in the front tyre of the car at the fork in the road.

I drew a gun. Then he drew a gun. So I drew my other gun. In no time at all, we were surrounded by drawings of guns.

I was a fishmonger for years but I gave it up. It's a sole-destroying job.

'Somebody's taken my place and I'm not happy!'
    'I don't see why. You told me you hate fish.'

'Do you believe in free speech?'
    'Certainly. It's the bedrock of democracy.'
    'Good. I'll just use your phone then.'

'Did you know there's mice in the police station, sergeant?'
    'Yeah, I know. I've always been a great believer in bringing back the cat.'

Jock's got a gay dog. It's a bit of a wag, really.

I met this intriguing girl. She was the India rubber woman at the local circus. I first met her when she was out stretching her legs.

'She's been on a massive charm offensive with the local butcher.'

'Aye, she's just playing for huge stakes.'

I met this cowgirl in what used to be termed 'the Wild West'. She was awfully bandy-legged and sadly, she didn't last long in the job. She got fired from this huge ranch in Wyoming. A shame, really, just because she couldn't keep her calves together.

Will you join me in a bowl of soup? I know it's a bit cramped but it's great fun!

'They call that woman over there who's blocking out the sun-light, the catapult.'

'Oh, why?'

'I believe it started when she first let herself go.'

My neighbour's a great carpenter. You know – sideboards, tables, chairs, he could make anything. One day his wife appeared in the garden with a dreadful hacking cough. I said to him, 'Your wife, is that her coughing?'

'Nah,' he replied, 'it's a rabbit hutch.'

CHIC'S GOBBLEDEGOOK GIBBERINGS

In a television interview with Tony Bilbo, Chic confessed that, from childhood onwards, he always secretly admired liars. Provided the story was perfectly outrageous (and, sometimes surreal), it was acceptable as long as it was told with utter conviction. Chic has been described as the original 'psychotic surrealist', but there is little doubt that in so much of his amazing anarchic comedic output, his 'off the wall' material, those many years ago, marked the genesis of what the media now call 'alternative humour'.

Are you growing a beard or just acting the goat?

Then there was this enormous bang! There was sand everywhere. Hurriedly, I filled the egg timer . . .

I hear he fell badly from the train. That was hard lines.

We have stained-glass windows. These damned pigeons!

Of course, *The Times* is a quality newspaper. See when you wrap your fish supper in it, the vinegar never seeps through.

That man plans to cross the Atlantic on a plank. Trouble is, he can't find one long enough.

'Why not do something, for once, for your country?'
   'Okay. What?'
   'Emigrate.'

It was so boring, six empty seats got up and walked out.

Looking at the obituary columns, it never fails to amaze me how people always die in alphabetical order.

A man entered a pet shop and asked to purchase a pet wasp.

'We don't stock pet wasps,' came the curt reply.

'That's funny! How come, then, you've got two in the shop window?'

Our closing-down sale's been such a success, we're opening up again on Monday.

'I do bird imitations,' Robin said to a prospective agent.

'Bird impressions? No, no. We've got plenty of them on the books already.'

'Please yourself,' said Robin, slightly miffed. Then he flew out the window.

'I do bird imitations. So it's nice to meet an agent like you.'

'Thank you. You do bird impressions? – maybe there's a different angle here we could project. Have you got a particular speciality? Whistling? Cackling? Maybe cawing?'

'No, no, no. I have to admit I'm just a wee bit of a beginner. But so far, I can eat worms no bother.'

'You didn't have the Rolling Stones in your day, Grandpa.'

'Aye, I suppose you're right, laddie, but we did have rickets, diphtheria and TB, so it kind of evens itself out.'

'Excuse me. Have you seen any police in the vicinity?' the stranger politely enquired.

'No, I have to say, I haven't seen any myself', I replied. Well, was I an idiot? He hammered me half-unconscious on the nut, just to run off with my wee wallet.

If something is neither here nor there, where the hell is it?

'Sergeant, did you hear my orders! Get those screaming women into my tent immediately!'

'But, sir, they're not screaming.'

'No back chat, Smith. They're not in my tent yet.'

I'm not often right, but it doesn't matter too much because I'm wrong again.

I was having a business lunch in my local Chinese restaurant when this cat exploded out of the kitchen and, like lightning, bolted straight out the door. I didn't say anything but I noticed 17 and 23 had been stroked off the menu.

I ordered spring chicken for breakfast. I didn't like it one bit! I kept getting springs in my teeth. But I should have taken the hint. That's the first time I've seen stomach pumps on every table.

Take my advice, dear – always wash your legs before a meal. You never know who's under the table.

Me, fit? Are you mad? I get winded playing draughts.

'Ah! But what have I got up my sleeve?'
   'A broken arm, if you're not careful.'

Did you notice the colour of her teeth when she decides to put them in?

This woman had a really slow Texan drawl. By the time she finished telling you about her past, you were part of it.

'Can I borrow your lawn mower?'
   'Sure, as long as you don't take it out of my garden.'

At the pictures last night, this stranger approached me. 'That's my seat,' he said.
   'Sorry,' I politely informed him, 'I got here first, and, no, no, I'm not budging.'
   'Och well, just please yourself,' said the interloper. 'I just hope you can play the organ.'

Mrs Smith, two doors up, keeps utterly silent about her age. But we know she's getting on. Last month I heard her birthday cake collapsed under the weight of the candles.

'Now I want you to leap from the Cessna aircraft at 3,000 feet. But, whatever you do, don't pull the ripcord until you're four feet from the ground. Is that quite clear now? Message understood?'

The trainee parachutist eyed the instructor incredulously 'Are you bleedin' kidding or something?'

'Why? What in God's name's the matter? Don't tell me you're scared of jumping a lousy four feet?'

Unfortunately, at a recent AGM of the Unspeakably Shy Society (Rutherglen Branch), nobody felt able to attend. None of them could face it.

Poor Jimmy suffers from paranoia and a dreadful inferiority complex. When the rest of his rugby side scrum down, he thinks they're all talking about him. I hear he's added a codicil to his will so that his hearse follows the other cars attending his funeral.

I wouldn't say she was a big girl. But I well recall once using her knickers for hang-gliding.

My wife gave me a present of an amazing atomic-powered watch that doesn't lose a single second in 10,000 years. And it comes with a three-month guarantee thrown in.

There's more nutrition in a prison sausage than in one and a half pounds of cardboard. They taste the same, of course.

'Do you believe in fairy godmothers?'
    'No. But we've got a fairy godfather. And I'm keeping a right good beady eye on him.'

'The bairn swallowed my fountain pen when you were out, dear.'

'Oh my God! What have you done about it, then?'

'Och! Don't get so worked up! It was OK – I just had to use a pencil.'

I wouldn't say I was a slow developer, but I suspect our teacher was quite pleased to have someone her own age in the class.

'I don't wish to be unkind, but, be honest, he was something of a freak.'

'Dear me, why do you say such a thing about the dear departed?'

'Well, why do you keep denying it? He had four arms, remember? Is that freakish or is it not?'

'Oh, I suppose you're right. And yet . . . how best to describe him? I suppose you could say, he was a man of many parts.'

'That's a very smart wristwatch you have, Terry.'

'Yes it is. And the good thing about it is you don't have to wind it.'

'Oh, is it one of those activated by the light or the motion of your wrist?'

'Not really. It's just a crap watch that's broken.'

She used to milk a cow until her eyesight got worse. Then she made one helluva mistake. The bull just kicked her teeth clean out.

I used to write her love letters in the sand. But it was an incredible hassle trying to get the sand into the post box.

'There's always a crowd following that villain.'

'Gosh! He must be very popular.'

'Popular indeed! They're all ruddy creditors!'

'Sit down! I'm going to tell you straight. I'm going to fling the cat out.'

'Why, for Heaven's sake?'

'It's on fire.'

'I'd like a two-carat diamond, set in a pendant, please, to match the colour of my eyes.'

'I regret to inform you, madam, no bloodshot diamonds have ever been found.'

'Did I know him? Of course I did! I was in the actual firing squad that shot him.'

'Funny, he didn't mention that.'

'No, he was quite a quiet lad really.'

'Waiter, kindly remove this ghastly fly from my soup.'

'Why sir?'

'Why! Why! You imbecile! Can't you see I want to dine alone!'

Little Red Riding Hood originally had nothing to do with kid's stories. He was a small but dangerous eighteenth-century Russian gangster.

'Do you approve of small families?'

'Very much so. My father was the youngest of eight midgets.'

Nellie, I'm sorry you're skint. Let's wander down to the pawnshop. That way I can get you alone.

I had this terrible dream of a fellow holding a knife at my throat. Luckily I woke up and there was this bloke wielding a knife at my throat which, of course, gave the dream terrific reality.

Three wise men entered a stable in Bethlehem when one of them stood on a rake which sprang forcefully up to belt him on the eye. 'Jesus Christ!' he yelled in pain.

'What a lovely name' said a young lady clutching an infant in swaddling clothes, 'and to think we were going to call him Wullie.'

'You're an Italian. Just bloody admit it!'

'No, I'm damned well not!' Many heated minutes of argument, then ensued . . .

'Och!' said the accused, eventually, 'If this is so important to you, then, yeah, yeah – please yourself! – fine, OK – I'm an Italian!'

'Ach!' said the other, magnanimously, 'I knew fine you were. However, I must admit, you don't look it!'

CHIC'S GOBBLEDEGOOK GIBBERINGS

Don't keep scratching! I've just swept up!

'I didn't know you bred bulldogs.'
    'What do you mean? That's my son!'

'Can you tell me if Alec Smith's here?'
    'Oh yes! You can't miss him. Take the second straitjacket on the right!'

I saw this advertisement for Hertz Van Hire. Some kind of Dutch artist, I suppose.

'I'm going to throw the towel in.'
    'Why? Are your boxer shorts falling down?'

I've often wondered . . . does an incubator chicken love its mother?

The lamplighters of Olde England
The lamplighters of our land,
You'll see them every evening
With their well trimmed wicks in hand!

Good evening, ladies and gentlemen. I'm your compère for the evening. I thought I'd mention that so that you don't have to dig your elbow into whoever's sitting next to you in a minute or two to ask, 'Who the hell is that?'

I never met an uglier man in my life. He actually looked like his passport photo.

I recently tried to entertain an audience of midgets. Unfortunately, it was a total flop. Every story I told them went clean over their heads.

This villain I know says crime doesn't pay but the hours are good. But he really can't help himself. Even the wool he pulls over your eyes is 50 per cent cotton and his favourite pastime is counting money in front of a mirror because he can't even trust himself.

The same villain read an advertisement 'Drink Canada Dry'. He was off to Canada like a shot but as he was about to embark on the ocean-going ship, he was arrested for picking his way through the crowd . . . one pocket at a time.

Do you like the suit I'm wearing? Look how it goes in at the waist [pointing at the waist]. Well it goes in again tomorrow.

Dad had died but his brother, 'Muttonhead', was still going strong as the black sheep of the family. Sadly, more recently, he had an empty, vacant smile. It should be OK though when his new teeth are ready.

I rented this flat in a dodgy area. It became clear there wasn't a single mouse in the apartment. They were all married. And the rooms were tiny! No kidding! – Even the mice were hunchbacked. I was told that on a clear day, I could see the sea. But the agent never mentioned that on a windy day I'd be in it!

I met this guy who had lived in the same house for thirty years. But that all changed. The Parole Board let him out.

My mother christened me Louis. I was the youngest of fourteen.

I once sat on a red-hot stove. I never felt a thing. It was around that time, I suppose, that they began to call me the 'Dead End Kid'.

When I left home, I slept in the gutter. It had its good points. I used to wake up in the groove and there was plenty room and running water.

'We've got a wonderful new line for bald-headed men.'

'Go on – tell me about it! What is it?'

'Bald-headed women.'

First sheep: Baaaah,

Second sheep: Mooooo.

First sheep: No! No! That should be a Baaaah!

Second sheep: Please! Can't you just let me do my own thing? I'm trying to learn a second language.

'Do you know algebra?'

'Sadly, no! I never got round to studying languages.'

'That three-year-old grey horse over there. Is it really only a three-year-old?'

'Aye, but it's an awful worrier.'

We live in a very nervous community. Even the dustbins get ulcers.

I met this guy who's a one-armed sculptor. He used to stick the chisel in his mouth and belt himself over the head with the mallet.

'You know, I knew a fellow who fell from a twenty-three storey building and yet incredibly he lived!'

'Wow! . . . That was nothing short of a miracle!'

'Not really. He fell from the ground floor.'

There was this terrific fire in the chorus girls' dressing room. It took a full five minutes to put the fire out and another four hours to get the firemen out.

I was knocked over twice by the same woman driver in the one day – once going forward and once reversing as she apologised.

'If everyone went around telling lies, where would we be?'

'Parliament, I suppose.'

'What a lovely dog. An Irish setter, is it? What's his name?'

'Thicko!'

'Oh, that's a little unfair. He's got a lovely coat and we can't all be Einsteins!'

'Well do you ken any other dog that chases parked cars?'

If at first you don't succeed, try, try, try and try again. Once you've done that, have the basic common sense to quit, you bampot!

Do you know how to fix a game? Well, you've got to start with loaded dice. But, if that doesn't work out – to rescue the situation – you've got to go for plan 'B', where you play snap for heavy money with a stutterer.

I knew this absent-minded streaker. He used to wonder why nobody paid any attention to him. It was simple really. He kept forgetting to take his clothes off.

I walked into my neighbour's house when he was ironing his shirt. I was just in time. His neck was badly burnt.

'Oh, it's lovely with all these clean-air restrictions to come across someone with a real coal fire.'

'I know. I wish I could bloody well light it.'

'How many sheep have you got, Hamish?'

'I honestly don't know. Every time I try and count them, I fall asleep!'

'I don't believe it! From these binoculars, it looks like the horse I've backed is going backwards!'

'Don't worry, Fred, you've backed it both ways.'

He was bone idle. Bone idle! Heavens, he was that lazy he married a pregnant woman.

We had this toy dog. It was a dachshund. Really cute wee thing. Sadly, one day it met its end as it wrapped itself round a sapling.

'Did you hear about Hetty Fraser?'

'No.'

'Wait till you hear this! She got sixty days in the slammer for plucking a turkey'.

'My goodness! That's surely excessive for removing its feathers. How did that come about?'

'She plucked it off the front butchery counter at the Co-op. The security got her.'

I went into this fancy store and held up the sales assistant with a price gun. 'Give me all the money in your till,' I said, 'or I'll mark down everything in the store!'

'We've put a little tinkly bell round our angel kitty's neck. That way we'll always know where the darling wee pussy might be.'

'Why go to so much trouble? Could you not just ram it in a drawer?'

'That Willie really loved his dog.'

'Away, I've seen him kicking the poor thing.'

'Ah! But remember! He always took his tackety boots off first.'

He was hellish mixed up, poor fellow. He had Dolly Parton for a mother but was bottle fed.

'That dirty old rag-bag is up before the court for interfering with young girls.'

'But wasn't he up once before for interfering with young boys?'

'Aye. That's right, so I suppose it's a step in the right direction.'

'Patrick, go down to the ironmonger on the corner and get me some cockroach powder.'

'OK, Mam. Gie me the money.'

'Here you are, and don't you be telling them what you want it for!'

I've got this extremely skinny bulldog. Actually, it used to be a whippet but it ran into a wall.

Jimmy always had that streak of rebellion. Even when he was born and the doctor gave him a slap, he turned round and slapped him straight back.

I was a happy baby. In fact, you could say I was always smiling. I had to, really. I'd swallowed a banana sideways.

Sonny celebrated his twenty-first birthday in Barlinnie Prison. As a special treat, he was granted a brief meeting with the governor where he asked (unfortunately without success) for the key of the door.

Have you got that new sci-fi book on space travel? It's supposed to be out of this world.

A chap fell out of a ten-storey building, and as a crowd gathered round, a policeman asked the badly injured man what had happened. 'I don't know myself,' he replied, 'I've only just got here.'

This cowboy rode into town on a cloud of dust. No horse, mind. Just a cloud of dust.

'My dad hasn't had a haircut now for close on ten years.'

'Sounds like he's a wee bit eccentric . . . '

'No no. He's as bald as a coot.'

First high-wire walker: Would you ever dare to work without a net?
Second high-wire walker: Good Heavens, no! My hair would be all over the place.

'Last time I saw you, you were in the Military Police.'

'Not exactly in. More between.'

'I didn't recognise you clean shaven. And, of course you've shrunk a good six inches. But it's nice to see you again Fred.'

'But my name's not Fred. It's Angus!'

'Oh! So you've changed your name as well!'

Two snakes met in the jungle. One asked, 'Excuse me. Please remind me, are we poisoners or constrictors?'

'We're poisoners, of course!' replied the other snake.

'Dammit! I thought so.' said the first. 'I've just bitten my lip.'

'I believe you're something of an expert on traditional Scottish airs.'

'Well, that's kind of you. I'd like to think I was. Och, aye!'

'Would you know *The Road to the Isles,* perhaps?'

'Of course.'

'Well, take it.'

'There's a helluva lot of jokes told in Glasgow that won't remotely get a laugh in London.'

'Why is that?'

'Well, they can't hear you.'

At the moment I'm living outside Glasgow. But if I behave myself, they might let me in.

'A single ticket to Buchanan Street Station, please.'

'We dinnae go near there, sir.'

'Well it says you do on the front of the bus!'

'Look, mister! There's a notice on the back that says "Persil washes whiter" but that disnae mean to say we take in washing!'

'And now we apologise for having to interrupt this programme to pass on an urgent message which has just been handed to me. It concerns all those who live in or around Port Glasgow. And the message reads: "'Hard luck!'"

Bob wasn't well liked. I remember one man took a pot-shot with a tomato at him at close range. Funny that! It missed him by miles and splattered all over me.

'How do you do? I've heard a lot about you. It's a pity you weren't there to defend yourself!'

There was a young girl from Australia
Who went to a dance as a dahlia.
But the petals revealed what they should have concealed
So the night and the dance were a failure.

I once kept a cat and a linnet. I've still got the cat but the linnet's in it.

'I'm very fond of porridge. As a woman officer, it's the second thing I have when I return home on leave.'
    'Is your husband like-minded, captain?'
    'Oh yes, we always start with grapefruit.'

She was quite shy, really, something of a doubter but also something of a 'goer'! She was only the daughter of a second-rate musician, but – by gum! – she knew Sir Henry Wood!

'Now, my darling, I hope you're not entertaining evil thoughts!'
    'Don't be daft, woman! They're entertaining me!'

I just love that drinking song from Handel's lager.

Have you heard that great new song that's rocketed into the Irish Top Twenty at number 36?

I knew this lovely lassie. Oh! She was magic! She had this smashing sports car and if she was in the mood – Carramba! – she could turn it into a quiet country lane.

'Do you know what happened during the night?'
    'Dunno.'
    'It got dark.'

How many times have I got to tell you? When the horse's eyes pop out, you should know you've tightened the straps far too much. And don't keep giving me that excuse that its neck's too fat!

His trouble was, he was too late to start earlier.

Yes, I know we've met before, but it doesn't change the fact that I want a fresh introduction.

This new aquarium is state of the art. It's got special blinds for shy fish.

Posh voice: 'Would you care for a dance?'

Chic: 'Oh, no thank you, but I'm grateful for being asked.'

Posh voice: 'Never mind and thank you for coming.'

Chic: 'Not at all. I thoroughly enjoyed myself.'

Posh voice: 'Goodnight to you.'

Chic: 'And, goodnight to you too, vicar.'

'If I buy a thousand currant buns from you for cash, I take it you'll give me a discount.'

'That all depends, sir. Are they for taking home or would you be eating them on the premises?'

'Can you fix my car, please? I think there's water in the carburettor.'

'No problem, sir. Where's the car parked?'
'In the Clyde.'

'How do I go about getting a car wash?'

'Just follow the instructions, Paddy. They're clearly printed on the wall over there.'

'Bejeezus! How did you know I was Irish?'

'We hardly ever get motorbikes in here.'

SCRUFFY, SHORT-HAIRED, AND OTHER SHAGGY-DOG STORIES

A North American Cherokee Red Indian stood on a street corner on Sauchiehall Street, Glasgow, feathery headdress flying above the war-paint. Every time a pretty woman passed, he raised his left hand and said 'When?' One day, a beautiful blonde shimmied past. He raised his hand as usual and repeated 'When?'

'How fascinating,' said the lady, addressing 'Big Kissing Cloud' with a plummy voice, 'because I thought all red Indians addressed people with "How!"'

'Me know how,' growled the Red Indian brave. 'Me only want to know when!'

I went to a hunt in my blue suit. It was terribly exciting, with dogs barking and horses whinnying. The lady of the manor told me to go into the big house, go down the corridor and enter the last door on the right. 'Oh,' I said, 'you've got me all wrong. I didn't come for *that* sort of thing.'

'Don't be silly,' she said, 'you can put on some riding clobber there!' I begged her pardon and returned in full hunt kit.

'Where are you from?' boomed the Hunt Master.

'Glasgow,' I replied.

'Good,' he said, 'you can have this Shettleston pony.'

Then it all started happening. Someone blew a bugle. (Either that, or he had an exceptionally long nose.) My pony embarrassed me terribly. It made me run alongside it but it soon lost me in the thrill of the chase. Unfortunately, I missed the kill as I still had a number of fields, ditches and fences to negotiate. But what a great day of sport!

A bachelor friend of mine visited the Ideal Home Exhibition at Olympia and bought an ironing board. It was a 'top of the range' ironing board which, handily, could be compressed into a small space and extended whenever required.

When he arrived at Euston for the return journey, he found that his sleeping compartment had mistakenly been allocated to others. To make matters worse, there was a current air strike on and the train was packed. The only option open to him was to share a four-berth second-class sleeper compartment with three others. He made his way up to his allocated bunk on the top and packed his ironing board neatly at the back.

He glanced idly round only to see a very attractive lady reclining in the bunk opposite. 'What's happened here?' he asked, 'I thought this was . . .'

'It's been absolutely dreadful,' the lovely girl interrupted, 'I had a first-class sleeper all to myself, but when I saw the chaotic state of the booking office, I'm just pleased, frankly, to be offered anything.'

My friend, not wanting to waste time and ignoring the two passengers below, smiled temptingly as he invited his new acquaintance over for a cigarette. 'I do have a flask of John Barleycorn, too,' he added under heavy-lidded eyes.

'Oh!' said his new friend demurely, 'but I don't even know you . . .'

'Don't let that worry you, dear,' he said reassuringly, 'I have a feeling we'll get on just fine.'

'Well, even if I did want to pop over to your bunk,' she said, 'I still couldn't manage it. I'd be disturbing the occupants of the bunks below and

I don't even know where that silly ladder's got to.'

'You don't need that silly ladder,' my friend assured her.

'I don't?' she enquired.

'No' he replied, 'I've got a little something here that can stretch over to your bunk. You can walk across, once I've got it up!'

This was all too much for one passenger below who had been 'lugging in' to their whispers 'I just don't bloody believe this!' he said in a raised voice, 'And, in any case, how's she going to get back?'

My wife Betty had a terrible accident when she was born. She lived. She was such an ugly child that when she entered a dark room, the dark screamed. Her mother taught her to sleep head-down covered in her pillow. This was in case she might terrify any unsuspecting burglar. Actually the two of us spent ten wonderfully happy years in Edinburgh. We both have warm, nostalgic memories of our time there. But then we met each other.

Our romance began as a blind date. 'I'll see

you at seven,' I told her on the phone.

'How will I know you?' she asked.

'I'll be wearing a yellow handkerchief in my inside pocket with a pair of matching Y-fronts,' I said.

We got married in a very simple ceremony, no fancy trimmings. Even the minister's name was the Rev. Smith. I caused a minor sensation by turning up in a white tie and tails. I clean forgot about trousers. The service was really a pretty private affair, just the four of us – me, Betty, the minister and the midwife. So then it was off to London for the honeymoon. Actually, I went on my own because it turned out Betty had been there before. And then, after the honeymoon, we settled down in our new home, where everything was brand new. I was kept awake every night listening to our contemporary furniture coming unstuck. But no sooner were we married than Betty began to put on an incredible amount of weight. She looked a bit like Jayne Mansfield and Sophia Loren all rolled into one huge, ugly, amorphous, shapeless lump. I'm not saying she was fat, but her belly and behind had to be given two different postcodes. She decided to go on a seafood diet – she only had to see it to eat it. But, oddly enough, she was a gifted sportswoman. She was captain, for instance, of the Inverkip Ladies Mud Wrestling team in the Sumo division. And she's still potty about bingo. She had a plaque made to fit above the fireplace which read, 'Bless this housey-housey.'

One night I came home and I could see she was very upset. She'd been having a bath in the afternoon – not a pretty sight at any time in the day, to be honest – when the doorbell rang.

'Who is it?' she bellowed.

'I'm a blind salesman,' came the reply.

'Come in, then,' she yelled, as she sat there unclothed like a bloated, beached Great White.

'Where do you want your blinds?' the salesman asked.

Last year I gave her a credit card, but she lost it. I haven't reported it because whoever found it is spending just a fraction of what she did. The other day, the two of us visited the waxworks. The attendants were very polite but they asked me, very nicely, to keep her moving about as they were stocktaking. And, of course, you have to be careful what you say to her sometimes. I once told her, for example, that I found black underwear a turn-on. She never washed my Y-fronts for a month and a half.

Mind you, I think there's something going on between the milkman and the wife. I sneaked down early one morning and kissed her on the back of her neck. 'We'll only need two pints this morning,' she said. And, only last week, she stayed out all night. When I asked her where she'd been, she said casually she'd stayed with the girl next door. Well, I knew she was lying! That's where I'd been.

And, then the in-laws . . . avoirdupois obviously runs in the family. Her mother's the fattest woman I've ever clapped eyes on. The only item of clothing she can buy ready-made and off the peg is a hankie. She's so fat that if she wants to turn over in bed, she has to get out and come back in again. Another huge fatty is her Auntie Fanny. She's got so many double chins that once when I went to kiss her, I got lost in the pleats.

The other day, I came home unexpectedly, only to catch the wife swinging the cat round and round and intermittently banging its head against the wall.

'What's the idea of treating the cat like that?' I shouted. Once she'd stopped revolving, she said, out of breath,

'When you were playing cards with your mates the other night. I heard you say quite distinctly that there was a right few quid in the kitty.'

Mind you, to be fair, she sticks to me through all the troubles I'd never have been in if I hadn't met her in the first place. But, at times, I get very depressed. One of my pals has encouraged me to drown my sorrows, and God knows, I've tried! But getting her massive body out of the house is a feat in itself so that getting her close to a stretch of water is a virtual impossibility.

Lady: Jeeves, I have to inform you that my long-term boyfriend returns after five years in India.

Butler: You had previously informed me, madam. No doubt he'll be very pleased to see you after such a long time.

Lady: Precisely. So do ring me the very moment he arrives.

One hour later, Cecil Carruthers-Ponsonby arrives to be greeted by the butler.

Cecil: Good to see you Jeeves. Is the Lady Mabel about? I'm sure she'll be anxious to meet me.

Butler: As a matter of fact, sir, your lady instructed me to inform her the moment you arrived.

Cecil: Jolly good! But I say, Jeeves, don't ring her just yet. After all, I've been away a long time, and I'm a teensy weensy bit nervous about what she might ask me.

Butler: Quite, sir. Ahem, I'd imagine the question uppermost in her mind is whether or not you consorted with other ladies while you were away, sir.

Cecil: Good Heavens, Jeeves! That's a bit of an awkward one. Bit of a fast ball, what?

Butler: I quite understand, sir. May I be so bold as to venture some advice? You see, if you're a little bit dubious and, let's suppose you decided to tell a tiny little fib, make it appear as the truth. That's vital. Don't hesitate. Be forthright! Come right out with it.

Cecil: Dammit, Jeeves! You're a bloody expert! How do you know all about it?

Butler: Well, I've been married for some

number of years, sir. Now, the first question she will ask is 'Have you been with any other girl?' You must be very dramatic and positive, answering, 'Darling, of course not. How could I?'

Cecil: Top hole, Jeeves! I must rehearse those lines. Darling, of course not. How could I? Darling, of course not. How could I? Darling, of course not. How could I?

Butler: That's it, sir. You've got the hang of it. Now I'll ring for m'lady.

Enter Lady Mabel, an English rose, a vision of loveliness . . .

Cecil: Mabel, darling! (As the butler discreetly withdraws)

Lady: Cecil! My own true love! Let me embrace you.

Then after a long and passionate clinch, she enquires, 'Do tell me, Cecil, while you were away, have you been faithful to me?'

Cecil: Darling, of course not. How could I?

A grotesquely ugly woman walked into a lounge bar in Argyle Street, Glasgow. Curiously, perched on her shoulder was a large parrot.

'If any man can guess what's on my shoulder,

I am all his – he can do whatever he wishes with me!' One old wag shouted from the far end of the bar,

'An elephant.'

Once the laughter had abated, the parrot lady said, 'That's near enough. I'm all yours!'

A man was walking his dog as it stopped, sniffed and peed on virtually every lamppost it passed. A policeman was watching. Eventually, he approached the dog-walker.

'I don't want to catch your dog pissing indiscriminately along the pavement again. If it must relieve itself, then drag it into the gutter. It's not only unhygienic, it's an affront to public decency. Otherwise, I'll throw the book at you.'

Two days later the policeman recognised the dog-walker he had previously chided, who now appeared to be in a distressed state. 'Good morning, sir. Where's your dog today? Did you leave him at home?'

'You and your walking him in the gutter! The poor dog's bloody well dead!' said the dog-walker. 'It died just walking him in the gutter.' Taken somewhat aback, the policeman enquired,

'How did it die walking in the gutter?' The dog-walker turned his back on the copper and shouted back, 'It fell off the bloody roof!'

Two pals had been meeting for years for a weekend drink in a pub just outside their village. Tam was a hunchback and Jock had a club foot. One night, when they were well-oiled, Tam said, 'The hell with it! Ah'm no for gawn the lang way hame the night. Ah'm gonna cut through the graveyard.'

'You're a braver man than me!' said Jock, 'but here – let me give you a leg up o'er the wall.' As Tam was making his way through the graveyard, a hooded mist-enshrouded apparition appeared and surveyed him.

'Here, you!' said the apparition. 'What's that on your back?'

'It's just a hump,' said Tam. At this the apparition approached him and effortlessly lifted it off.

The following weekend, the two friends met as usual in the pub and Jock was astounded to see Tam's hump had gone. After Tam treated his pal to the whole story, Jock mused, 'Maybe,

Tam, if I took a dander through the graveyard, maybe the ghostie would get rid of ma club foot. Dammit! It's worth a shot anyway!'

'Go yersel',' said Tam. 'But once was enough for me. But Ah'll gie ye a leg-up o'er the wa', the same as ye did fer me.'

Sure enough, as Jock was making his way through the graveyard, the apparition again materialised.

'Here, you!' the apparition said. 'What's that on your back?'

'Nothin',' said Jock.

'Well, here's a hump for you then.'

A priest was walking through a little market town some miles from his country parish on his day off. He felt a bit hungry, so he went to a small restaurant in a back street. He ordered steak, but not too well done. After the meal, he thanked the restaurateur and told him how much he'd enjoyed the steak.

'Thank you, Father,' said his host, 'and next time you're in just ask for a bloody steak and I'll know it's you and exactly what you want.' Three weeks later the priest was having another day off and happened to mention to his bishop that he was returning to the little market town with its restaurant that served tasty steaks.

'That's a place I've never been,' said the bishop. 'Do you mind if I join you?' So the priest took the bishop to the wee restaurant. He placed the order for his companion and himself. 'Could you give us two bloody steaks, please?' At this the bishop exclaimed, 'Oh! I just love this informality, Father! Waiter, could we have two fucking great helpings of chips as well, please?'

A drunk walked up to the ticket office in Central Station, Glasgow and bought a single ticket to Ayr. He staggered up platform one singing 'The Star o' Rabbie Burns', where the ticket inspector told him, 'Sorry, sir, wrong platform. Try platform nine.' Still belting out 'The Star o' Rabbie Burns', the drunk staggered round to platform nine. There the ticket inspector informed him that the Ayr train had been diverted to platform twelve. Still giving 'The Star o' Rabbie Burns' laldie, he got to platform twelve and fell into the train. But, unfortunately he was seated next to a Wee Free minister who viewed him with disgust as alcoholic fumes wafted around him. 'You are the work of the devil, you drunken, evil man!' the minister berated him. 'Don't you realise you're on the road to hell?'

'Ah, fer the love o' the wee man, is this no murder?' said the drunk. 'Ah'm in the wrong train again!'

In many ways, I had a wonderful family life as a child. We could have been featured on *Happy Families* any time. But I don't think my parents liked me from the word 'go'. . . at least, to begin with. They used to make me wear a label round my neck, but with someone else's address on it. The worst day was the day that they sent me out. When I got back, they'd moved. But I must say this! There was no trace of insanity in our family. Far from it! – we had baths every day and me and my three sisters had endless fun playing snakes and ladders on Granny's varicose veins. And then my cousin had a shape like Marilyn Monroe. (Actually, it was a wee bit embarrassing for me. He was a boy.)

But, oh! The family! For example, my grand-father was a stuntman in Hollywood, so we never saw much of him. He used to have one foot, bareback, on two horses, and he did it just fine. Then, one day, he came to a fork in the road. Now, these days, we hardly see him at all.

My parents were wonderful! And they were always that ready to compromise. One of my sisters wanted a cat for a pet and I wanted a dog. It was wonderful, really. Yes, they bought my sister a cat but the thoughtful thing was that they taught it to bark. And my dad kept a scrapbook. In it, he recalled all the most memorable fights he had with mother. And, since he used to eat like a horse, the nosebag my mum got him made a huge difference to the hoovering. He was a very religious man, though. For example, he had all Sydney Divine's records. And he had this tender streak of kindness – he would walk me to school every morning. I suppose it was handy, him being in the same class. When, eventually, Dad got a job, he used to say he was in the meat packing business – he worked in a corset factory. And there was one great thing about the family – there were no favourites. No, no. There was no taking sides. Dad just hated the lot of us.

When jobs were plentiful, we ate like kings.

One Christmas our turkey was so big we'd to get an upholsterer to stuff it. When things were not so good, I heard my mother say to a neighbour, 'I can't blether all day. I'd better get a crust on that pie before my man comes home and sees what's in it!' One day, at what was probably our lowest ebb, mother announced there was good news and bad news. 'The bad news,' she declared, 'is that there's only pigswill for dinner. But the good news is – there's not enough to go round.'

The ultimate luxury in our house at that time was ashtrays without advertisements, and it was all the wolf could do to keep us away from his door. We dreamt of the day we could paper behind the cuckoo clock and, of course, we didn't have to bother with carpets as we had wall-to-wall mildew. It was the only house I can recall that had guttering inside. I remember a luxury meal consisted of prairie sandwiches – two wedges of bread with wide open spaces in between. At one really dreadful time, we were forced to drink skimmed water and there were so many holes in my socks I could put them on sixteen different ways.

But I'll never forget my dear mum. I always held the door open for her when she went out to do her paper round. And she was so house proud that when my dad got up at night to sleepwalk, she had made the bed by the time he got back. She was daft on cleanliness, too. When a cigarette commercial came on the telly, she put an ashtray under the set and she dusted everything, even the tropical fish.

My sisters were brought up very strictly. They weren't allowed to turn the cat over until they were thirteen. Oh, but they made up for it since. One of my sisters has been married that many times she's bought a drip-dry wedding dress. Another sister has five children. 'Why don't you marry the father?' I keep asking her. 'I don't like him,' she tells me.

Just before the start of a horse race, a punter saw a priest sprinkle holy water over a horse. To his astonishment, it won by eight lengths at 4 to 1. Over the next few races, he couldn't help watching the priest sprinkling his water on one improbable winner after another. Now – in the last race – the punter decided to get in on the act.

He hammered every penny he had on the horse to win after watching the priest identify his selection with the holy water. Halfway through the race, however, tragedy struck and the horse he'd backed pulled up and promptly dropped dead. The punter was full of righteous indignation, 'What the hell happened there, Father?' the punter demanded. 'You put water on all the other horses and they won. But that last one dropped down dead. Dead as a dodo! And worse than that, that was the horse I was betting on.'

'I take it you're not a Roman Catholic, my son?'

'No! But what's that got to bloody do with it?'

'You are unable,' the priest replied, ' to distinguish between blessing a horse and giving it the last rites.'

A small Jewish boy was continuously told by his rabbi that if he thought dirty, evil thoughts, he would turn to stone. One day, on holiday in London, he ventured into Soho. Mischief and curiosity got the better of him and he sneaked into a strip club . . . but not for long! After five minutes, half hysterical, the boy ran for the front door, screaming. But the doorman grabbed him and demanded to know what was wrong. Breathless, the boy blurted out, 'My rabbi said that if I had dirty thoughts, I would turn to stone! Well, it's started!'

Two Irish navvies were digging a trench outside the local brothel. Pat turned to Mick, 'That's a terrible place. Just look at those half-naked brazen hussies!'

After a while, they spotted a minister sneak round the corner and furtively scan the area to avoid recognition. Then, into the brothel he went.

'Is that not dreadful, Mick?' said Pat. 'And him supposed to be a man of God. But what else can you expect of a Protestant?'

Then, half an hour later, they spied a rabbi skulking into the same doorway.

'Did you get an eyeful of that, Mick?' Pat asked. 'And a rabbi too. Me? I would never trust a man with a beard.'

After a while, a car drew up beside the brothel and a priest skipped in through a side entrance.

'Would you look at that, Patrick?' said Mick

admiringly. 'What a brave man going into that den of iniquity to reform those unholy sluts!'

'Yes, Mick, and t'ink o' all the confessions the poor man will be forced to listen to!'

Following a daring bank raid, the police made public appeals for any information from witnesses which might assist in tracing and convicting the thief or thieves. For five days, the police had no leads and then a man appeared at a nearby police station.

'I'm here about the recent bank robbery. I know what you should be looking for – it's an elephant, not a bloke.'

'Och! Don't be daft, sir! An elephant! Aye, that'll be right,' the duty sergeant said sarcastically.

'I'm telling you!' countered the alleged witness. 'I saw it! It was an elephant!'

The officer sighed deeply and opening his notebook to humour the lunatic. He asked resignedly, 'OK, sir, let's begin by describing the elephant. Was it an African or Indian elephant?'

'How the hell would I know?' the witness replied. 'It was wearing a stocking over its head.'

The slave master shouted at his galley slaves as he cracked his whip for attention. 'I have good and bad news for you today. First, the good news. You will be unshackled and free to walk around the galley until early afternoon. You will also receive extra rations at lunch time. And now for the bad news. The captain wants to go water skiing this afternoon.'

A circus came to town and the acrobat went to the local chapel for confession. After the recently appointed priest had listened intently and discovered what the chap did for a living, he said, 'My goodness! It's years since I was at a circus. Could you do some tricks for me?'

'Certainly,' said the acrobat and he began to do handstands, somersaults, back flips and cartwheels up and down the aisle. But two elderly ladies had entered the chapel and witnessed the bizarre scene.

'My God! That's way too much for me. If that's the new man's idea of penance,' said one old dear, 'I'm off to join the Proddies!'

A minister, doing his hospital rounds, visiting the parishioners in the ward, was approached by one of the sisters. 'Father, would you mind visiting the wee Chinaman at the end of the ward? He's in a bad way, I'm afraid.'

The minister found the Oriental gentleman lying poorly in bed wearing an oxygen mask. 'How are you, my son?' he enquired. The Chinaman turned red and mumbled at him, waving his arms frantically. 'I don't understand. All I asked you was how are you, my son?' At this the patient turned a deep purple and started a muffled babbling. 'Sorry. I still can't make you out,' said the minister, anxiously. In desperation, the Chinaman grabbed a pen and paper and wrote something down before turning black and, after some violent shuddering, collapsed stone dead in the bed. The reverend sought out the ward sister. 'I'm afraid the Chinese gentleman has just died,' he told her, 'but before he passed away, he wrote me a note. Unfortunately, I don't read Mandarin Chinese.'

'Luckily, I do,' said the sister. 'Let me see. Oh! Dear God! It reads: "You stupid bastard, you're standing on my oxygen supply!"'

The victim of a house fire was lucky to be alive. The fire brigade heroically rescued him just in the nick of time but his two wooden legs were burnt to a cinder. After a period of recovery in hospital for treatment for shock and smoke inhalation, he contacted his insurance company where he had cover for fire damage. However it came as a further shock to hear from the insurance company a week after he had lodged his claim, that compensation had been refused as he didn't have a leg to stand on.

Two priests were on a plane to Rome and halfway there, the pilot switched on the intercom. 'Good afternoon, ladies and gentlemen. Sorry to trouble you, but we have an emergency and I would appeal to you not to panic. The aircraft has suffered from a vital electrical failure in the cockpit. We may have to ditch the aircraft in the sea. Will you please, now, put on your life jackets and I repeat, please try and stay calm! Thank you.'

One priest turned to the other, 'We'd better hear each other's confession before it's too late. I'll go first. I've been a heavy smoker and drinker and I've had congress with nearly every woman, married and single, in my parish.'

The other priest said, 'I wish to confess I'm a raving alcoholic and I can't resist tampering with small boys.'

Just then, however, the intercom was switched back on. 'Good afternoon, ladies and gentlemen, once more. It's all good news. The back-up emergency supply of electricity has kicked in and the emergency is officially over. Please enjoy the rest of your flight.'

At this, one priest turned to the other, commenting, 'Isn't it amazing the lies you tell when you're really scared!'

A wee boy was walking down the Main Street with a bottle of sulphuric acid in his hand when a priest spotted him. 'My goodness, laddie! That's exceedingly dangerous stuff for a small boy to be carrying. Give it to me this very minute.'

'Ah!' said the wee boy, 'but whit are you going to gi'e me for it in exchange, Faither?' The priest reached into his inside pocket and brought out a small bottle of fluid.

'I'll give you this bottle of holy water.'

'Whit guid does that dae?' asked the boy.

'Well,' said the priest, 'once I sprinkled this over one of a lady parishioner's stomach and it came to pass that she brought forth a baby.'

'Och! That's nothin' Faither. I sprinkled this over a cat's arse and it overtook an E-type Jaguar!'

An earnest and apprehensive young man was told at his initial instruction of the strict and solemn vows of his chosen monastic order. One of the strictest vows was that of silence, and he learnt that he would be permitted to speak only once every five years and then, only for a minute. After five years had elapsed, the young monk stood up at the refectory table and said, 'There's not enough salt in the porridge.' He then sat down again in silence. Five years on, he got up once more. 'There's still not enough salt in the porridge,' whereupon he recommenced his compulsory silence for another five years. Month by dreary month and year by interminable year, another five years came eventually to pass. He stood up for the third time and said, 'Your porridge is still rotten and I'm leaving!'

'Thank God!' said the Father Abbot. 'You've done nothing but moan since you came here.'

'Excuse me. I don't wish to be personal, but is there any insanity in your family?'

'No. Absolutely not! . . . Except . . .'

'Except what? You hesitated there, Andy.'

'Well maybe my brother's a little odd.'

'Do tell me. Is he merely idiosyncratic or is he off his rocker, to put it bluntly?'

Andy sighed heavily. 'Well, it's hard to say. You see, he thinks he's a chicken!'

'A chicken! A chicken! What on earth are you playing at? Why is he not receiving some form of therapy or treatment in an appropriate institution?'

'Well, we did think of that but we need the eggs.'

Two elderly men had been bowlers all their lives Both aged sixty-seven, they had won all the local honours available to them. One day one of them conjectured, 'Bob, I wonder if they have bowling greens in heaven?' The other replied, 'Well, Jim, I don't know about that. But let's make a pact that whoever dies first comes back and tells the other.'

It was not long thereafter that Jim died. Bob waited patiently for a message but he heard nothing for the next six months. Then he and his wife went on holiday and on the third day at their hotel, Bob went for a walk in the woods nearby. Suddenly a deep, booming voice – but with Jim's unmistakable accent – greeted him, 'Hello, Bob,' the voice said.

'Oh! My God! It's you, Jim. Wonderful to hear from you at long last.'

'Yes, Bob, and let me tell you, they have utterly magnificent bowling greens up here. And, guess what? You're down for a tournament next week!'

A priest had just taken confession at a convent and the Mother Superior saw him to the door. 'Well, Reverend Mother, it's such a lovely God-given day. I'm going to shed my dog collar and play a round of golf.'

'Oh!' said the Mother Superior,' how exciting! Do you know, it's a game I've never seen played. Could I possibly join you?'

'Certainly,' he replied and off to the golf

course they went. He teed up at the first hole and, with an air shot, missed the ball completely.

'Fuck it!' he exclaimed.

'Father, please – would you kindly moderate your language?'

The priest apologised and the round continued. However at the third hole, playing his second shot to the green, he sliced his ball into a deep bunker.

'Oh! Fuck it!' he cursed again.

'Father! What have I told you?' said his companion.

'I really am sorry, Reverend Mother. I won't do it again. May the Lord strike me down dead if I do!'

Tragically, after an incident-free remaining round of golf, the priest missed a short easy putt on the eighteenth. Losing his self-control, and in front of the clubhouse, he roared out, for the last time, 'Fuck it!'

Instantly a bank of black clouds appeared overhead and then they parted when, all of a sudden, a giant fork of lightning flashed and crackled down, searing the grass within inches of the priest's foot. Then came the rumble of a deep resonant voice from the heavens, 'Missed . . . Fuck it!'

A red-hot Orangeman was really hurt and angry at his little boy, who began to flunk all his classes at school. Gradually his marks got worse and worse until he was finally expelled from three separate, but famous, Ulster Protestant schools. With huge misgivings, the Orangeman in desperation entered the boy in a private Roman Catholic school.

Six months went by. The wee lad had perfect attendance, perfect behaviour and had kept himself neat and tidy. And, best of all, his end of term marks had improved one hundred per cent.

The Orangeman was really surprised – and enraged! – by this, and collared his son one night. 'What's the carry-on here?' he demanded to know. 'I sent you to good Protestant schools and you messed up everything! Then I send you to this Catholic school and a complete change comes over you! Explain yourself, boy!'

'Well, Dad, it's like this. They've got this poor bloke nailed to a cross and I'm bloody terrified I'm going to be next!'

The Mother Superior rose one morning, and as she walked through the convent to breakfast a nun, passing her in the corridor, said, 'Good morning, Reverend Mother. I see you got up on the wrong side of the bed this morning.'

This puzzled her, but she let it pass. However, two minutes later another nun passed by, 'Good Morning, Reverend Mother, I see you got up on the wrong side of the bed this morning.'

Now she was perplexed and vexed, but again she let it pass until she arrived at the entrance to the dining hall, where a third nun addressed her in identical fashion. This stopped her in her tracks and she indicated to the nun to stop. 'Sister,' she said, 'you are the third person to say this to me this morning and I can't think why. Would you please enlighten me?'

'Certainly, Reverend Mother. You have Father Murphy's boots on.'

In the Middle Ages, three pregnant nuns were hauled in front of the Mother Superior. Addressing them, she intoned, 'This is a mortal sin and all three of you are condemned to die according to the works of whoever impregnated you. Let this be an example to any other sister who wishes to defy their vows of chastity.' Turning to the first accused she demanded to know who was responsible.

'A fireman, Reverend Mother.'

'So be it. You will suffer death by burning at the stake. Take her away!'

She turned to the second fallen nun. 'What was the work of your child's father?'

'A stone mason, Reverend Mother, but I pray you, have mercy!'

'Take her away. She shall be stoned to death. Bring forth the third sinner.'

The nun, dishevelled and in a state of distress, was arraigned before her.

'I demand to know what occupation your lover pursued?'

'A jockey, Reverend Mother.'

Two men were talking in a Chinese takeaway as they waited for their order to be served. 'I've always been puzzled,' said one, 'that although we all know of Russian, American, French even Russian Jews, you never hear of Chinese Jews, do you?'

'That's right. I never thought about that,' his friend replied, 'I'll ask the waiter. Excuse me, do you have Chinese Jews?'

'Wait a moment, please, sir. I will make enquiries.'

Some minutes later, the waiter returned. 'Velly solly, sir. We have no Chinese Jews, only orange, lime or lemon.'

A priest attending an ecumenical council in the City Chambers began to get bored by the speeches, and even more so by the dinner and subsequent socialising. He started to converse with a Wee Free Minister. After a general chat the priest asked the minister if he would like a brandy. 'Och! Lord no. I'm not into the evils of drink, myself. No, I'd prefer a good woman.'

'What an excellent idea!' said the priest. 'I hadn't realised we have a choice!'

A medical missionary in dense jungle in Papua New Guinea met a huge colossus of a man who must have been 7ft 6in tall, weighing upwards of 30 stone. Once he established that the colossus could speak English, he said, 'I can't help commenting on your magnificent size. What's your diet?'

'Beans, sir.'

'What? Runner beans, green beans, soya beans? Tell me!'

'Just beans, sir.'

'Don't tell me! Heinz Beans?'

'Way out, man . . . human beans.'

A man with a serious heart condition won £250,000 on the pools, and because of his health his wife was too frightened to break the news to him in case he had a seizure. She explained the situation to her local minister. 'Don't worry,' he said. 'I'll call round and break the news very gently to him.' One hour later, he arrived. He sat down to have a lengthy discussion with the husband as his wife discreetly left the room. Then, craftily, he posed a hypothetical question to the pools winner. 'What would you do, Alec, if you won £250,000 on the pools?'

'Oh, that's an easy one! I'd keep half and give the other half to you and the Church.' The shock was too much for him. The minister dropped down dead.

The local minister was busy doing the rounds of his parish. He happened upon Ahmed, a Christian of Asian origins. 'How nice to see you, Ahmed! Have you found a job yet?'

'Great news, Reverend Sir, I'm going to be working full time with Cheesus.'

'Oh! That's wonderful. There is nothing more rewarding than working for the Lord Jesus.'

'No, no, Reverend Sir, Cheddar "Cheesus".'

A motorist drove frantically into the city zoo, where he located the Head Keeper. 'What's the average height of penguins?' he demanded in a panic.

'Two to three feet tall, sir. But that all depends on the breed.'

'Oh! My God!' said the motorist. 'I was fearing the worst!'

'What's upsetting you sir? You're clearly overwrought.'

'So would you be,' replied the distraught driver. 'I've just run over two nuns!'

Two roofers were working on the slates of a chapel when one had a sneezing fit during which his dentures flew out and dropped through an open skylight. 'Ah've lost ma wallies doon that skylight,' said the unlucky roofer.

'Well, get doon the scaffolding and get the priest. I spied him coming in,' said his work mate.

Gingerly, he made his way back down and entered the chapel. 'Have you seen a set o' wallies, sir?' he said to the priest. 'Ah sneezed them doon the skylight.'

'Oh, yes. I'm pleased to say, I found them,' said the priest. 'They were caught in one of the urinals.'

'Thanks a million, sir,' said the roofer as he slammed the dentures back into his mouth. On getting back up on the roof, his pal asked him if he'd been successful.

'Yeah,' said the now toothed-up roofer, 'he found them in a urinal. By the way, what's a urinal?'

'How the hell would I know?' replied the other. 'I'm not a Catholic!'

A woman whose husband was a raving alcoholic answered a knock on the door. Two crew-cut but smart Americans stood there, and one addressed her, 'Good evening, Mrs McCafferty, may God bless you! We're both missionaries from the Mormon Church in Salt Lake City, Utah in the US of A.' Gesturing towards his colleague he continued, 'This is Elder Smith and I'm Elder Brown.'

The 'wifie' pointed at her drunken husband stretched out on the couch in a semi-comatose condition. 'Aye,' she said, 'well ye'd better come in an' meet yer comrade in drink, Eldorado!'

Three wee boys were walking by a river in full spate when they saw a man in great difficulty and in danger of drowning. Selflessly, they jumped into the water, and with a broken bough from a tree they managed to save the poor wretch. After some time, when the man had recovered sufficiently, he thanked the boys profusely. 'My sons,' he said, 'I am a bishop in the Holy Roman Catholic Church, and to show my gratitude to you, if I can, I will try and realise your dearest wish.'

'Well,' said the first lad, 'I'd like to go to Lourdes, please, to pray to keep my family in good health.'

'How delightful!' said the bishop. 'Your unselfish wish is granted.' The next wee boy asked for a meeting with the Holy Father in Rome. This wish, too, was granted. Then, turning to the third laddie, he asked, 'And what about you, young man?'

'I'd like a state funeral, please, sir.'

'A state funeral? Why on earth would a boy like you of such tender years want a state funeral?'

'Och, that's easy,' said the wee fellow. 'The minute my father finds out who I've saved from drowning, he'll murder me!'